# FIVE SPECKLED FROGS

Retold by STEVEN ANDERSON

Illustrated by TIM PALIN

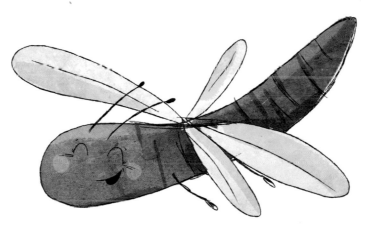

## CANTATA
### LEARNING

WWW.CANTATALEARNING.COM

## CANTATA LEARNING

Published by Cantata Learning
1710 Roe Crest Drive
North Mankato, MN 56003
www.cantatalearning.com

Library of Congress Control Number: 2015932798
Anderson, Steven
    Five Speckled Frogs / retold by Steven Anderson; Illustrated by Tim Palin
    Series: Sing-along Math Songs
    Audience: Ages: 3–8; Grades: PreK–3
    Summary: In this classic song, five very hungry frogs are sitting on a very
special log eating some most delicious bugs.
    ISBN: 978-1-63290-384-6 (library binding/CD)
    ISBN: 978-1-63290-515-4 (paperback/CD)
    ISBN: 978-1-63290-545-1 (paperback)
    1. Stories in rhyme. 2. Counting—fiction. 3. Frogs—fiction.

Book design and art direction, Tim Palin Creative
Editorial direction, Flat Sole Studio
Music direction, Elizabeth Draper
Music arranged and produced by Mark Oblinger

Printed in the United States of America in North Mankato, Minnesota.
122015    0326CGS16

Frogs have long, sticky tongues. They use their tongues to catch bugs to eat. Count down from five as the frogs **leap** into the water after a **dragonfly**.

To see if they catch the dragonfly, turn the page and sing along!

Five green and **speckled** frogs sat on a speckled log eating some most **delicious** bugs. Yum! Yum!

One jumped into the pool where it was nice and cool.

Then there were four green and speckled frogs.

Four green and speckled frogs sat on a speckled log eating some most delicious bugs. Yum! Yum!

One jumped into the pool
where it was nice and cool.
Then there were three green
and speckled frogs.

Three green and speckled frogs sat on a speckled log eating some most delicious bugs. Yum! Yum!

One jumped into the pool where it was nice and cool.
Then there were two green and speckled frogs.

Two green and speckled frogs sat on a speckled log eating some most delicious bugs. Yum! Yum!

One jumped into the pool where it was nice and cool.
Then there was one green and speckled frog.

One green and speckled frog sat on a speckled log eating some most delicious bugs. Yum! Yum!

One jumped into the pool where it was nice and cool.
Then there were no green and speckled frogs.

Don't you wish those five green and speckled frogs would get back on their speckled log?

One green and speckled frog jumped onto the log.
Then there was one green and speckled frog.

Another speckled frog jumped onto the log.
Then there were two green and speckled frogs.

And one more speckled frog jumped onto the log.
Then there were three green and speckled frogs.

And another speckled frog jumped onto the log.
Then out of the water leaped the last green frog.

Five green and speckled frogs sat on a speckled log eating some most delicious bugs. Yum! Yum!

# SONG LYRICS
## Five Speckled Frogs

Five green and speckled frogs sat on a speckled log eating some most delicious bugs. Yum! Yum!

One jumped into the pool where it was nice and cool. Then there were four green and speckled frogs.

Four green and speckled frogs sat on a speckled log eating some most delicious bugs. Yum! Yum!

One jumped into the pool where it was nice and cool. Then there were three green and speckled frogs.

Three green and speckled frogs sat on a speckled log eating some most delicious bugs. Yum! Yum!

One jumped into the pool where it was nice and cool. Then there were two green and speckled frogs.

Two green and speckled frogs sat on a speckled log eating some most delicious bugs. Yum! Yum!

One jumped into the pool where it was nice and cool. Then there was one green and speckled frog.

One green and speckled frog sat on a speckled log eating some most delicious bugs. Yum! Yum!

One jumped into the pool where it was nice and cool. Then there were no green and speckled frogs.

Don't you wish those five green and speckled frogs would get back on their speckled log?

One green and speckled frog jumped onto the log. Then there was one green and speckled frog.

Another speckled frog jumped onto the log. Then there were two green and speckled frogs.

And one more speckled frog jumped onto the log. Then there were three green and speckled frogs.

And another speckled frog jumped onto the log. Then out of the water leaped the last green frog.

Five green and speckled frogs sat on a speckled log eating some most delicious bugs. Yum! Yum!

# Five Speckled Frogs

**World**
Mark Oblinger

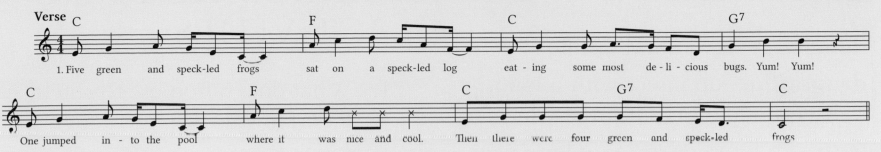

**Verse**

1. Five green and speck-led frogs sat on a speck-led log eat - ing some most de - li - cious bugs. Yum! Yum! One jumped in - to the pool where it was nice and cool. Then there were four green and speck-led frogs

**Verse 2**
Four green and speckled frogs sat on a speckled log
eating some most delicious bugs. Yum! Yum!
One jumped into the pool where it was nice and cool.
Then there were three green and speckled frogs.

**Verse 3**
Three green and speckled frogs sat on a speckled log
eating some most delicious bugs. Yum! Yum!
One jumped into the pool where it was nice and cool.
Then there were two green and speckled frogs.

**Verse 4**
Two green and speckled frogs sat on a speckled log
eating some most delicious bugs. Yum! Yum!
One jumped into the pool where it was nice and cool.
Then there was one green and speckled frog.

**Verse 5**
One green and speckled frog sat on a speckled log
eating some most delicious bugs. Yum! Yum!
One jumped into the pool where it was nice and cool.
Then there were no green and speckled frogs.

**(Spoken)**
Don't you wish those
five green and speckled frogs
would get back on their speckled log?

**Outro (1-3)**

1. One green and speck-led frog jumped on - to the log. Then there was one green and speck-led frog.

**Outro 2**
Another speckled frog jumped onto the log.
Then there were two green and speckled frogs.

**Outro 3**
And one more speckled frog jumped onto the log.
Then there were three green and speckled frogs.

4. And an-oth - er speck-led frog jumped on - to the log. Then out of the wa - ter leaped the last green frog.

5. Five green and speck-led frogs sat on a speck-led log eat - ing some most de - li - cious bugs. Yum! Yum!

# GLOSSARY

**delicious**—very good tasting

**dragonfly**—an insect with a long, thin body and four large wings

**leap**—to jump or spring a long way

**speckled**—covered with small dots or patches of color

# GUIDED READING ACTIVITIES

1. What does a frog use to catch flies? How do you use your tongue?

2. Frogs are green. Can you think of other things that are green?

3. Dragonflies are not dragons. They are beautiful insects. Draw a dragonfly. How many wings do you have to make?

## TO LEARN MORE

Dickmann, Nancy. *A Frog's Life*. Mankato, MN: Heinemann-Raintree, 2011.

Hassett, Ann. *Too Many Frogs*. New York: HMH Books for Young Readers, 2011.

Pixton, Kaaren. *Plip-Plop Pond!* New York: Workman Publishing, 2010.

Sweeney, Alyse. *Frogs*. Mankato, MN: Capstone Press, 2010.